The Story of a Special Day
Volume 78

March 18

77th day of the year
(78th in leap years)
288 days remaining
until the end of the year.

by Michael Dobson

Timespinner
Press

Table of Contents

Cover: Waikiki Beach and Diamond Head, Hawaii, for the Event of the Day.

Back Cover: The month of March, from the French Gothic illuminated manuscript *Les Très Riches Heures du duc de Berry.*

March 18 Quotations

"We take our bearings, daily, from others. To be sane is, to a great extent, to be sociable."

— *John Updike, born March 18, 1932*

"There are different flavours of sexiness."

— *Queen Latifah, born March 18, 1970*

"Armed conflict between nations is a nightmare to me, but if I were convinced that any nation had made up its mind to dominate the world by fear of its force I should feel it should be resisted."

— *Neville Chamberlain, born March 18, 1869*

"Man is born as a freak of nature, being within nature and yet transcending it. He has to find principles of action and decision-making which replace the principles of instincts."

— *Erich Fromm, died March 18, 1980*

"Without heroes, we're all plain people, and don't know how far we can go."

— *Bernard Malamud, died March 18, 1986*

Event of the Day

Hawaii Statehood Bill Signed

On March 18, 1959, President Dwight D. Eisenhower signed the Hawaii Admissions Act, which dissolved the Territory of Hawaii and established the State of Hawaii as the 50th state in the United States of America.

Hawaii's journey to American statehood was surprisingly rocky. The Hawaiian Islands were first settled by Polynesians between 300 and 800 CE. First contact with Europeans came in 1778, when Captain James Cook, a British explorer, discovered the Hawaiian archipelago (which he called the "Sandwich Islands" after the Earl of Sandwich) while on his way to North America. On his way back, Cook stopped on the island of Hawai'i, staying a month in order to make some much needed repairs to his ships. During that time, some Hawaiians took one of his smaller boats. In return, Cook tried to take the King of Hawai'i hostage. A fight broke out, and Cook was killed on February 14, 1779.

The Hawaiians learned much from Cook, and soon King Kamehameha I launched a military campaign to conquer the other islands in the chain, establishing the Kingdom of Hawai'i in 1810. He was not the only person with designs on the islands. Located roughly halfway across the Pacific between the Americas and Asia, Hawaii was of great strategic importance, not least because the two best harbors were located on the island of Oahu: Honolulu Harbor and Pearl Harbor. The British occupied Hawaii for six months in 1843. The French invaded in 1849. But the end of the Kingdom of Hawai'i came about in 1893, when local businessmen, supported by U.S. Marines, overthrew Queen Lili'uokalani and lobbied for the United States to annex the islands. The subsequent Republic of Hawai'i lasted only until 1898, when the U.S. formally annexed the islands and created the Territory of Hawai'i.

Congress began to consider Hawaiian statehood as early as 1935, but politicians from the American South objected because of race: Hawaii would be the first American state with a non-white majority. In 1940, Hawaiians voted overwhelmingly in favor of statehood, but the matter was postponed after Pearl Harbor and not taken up again until after the end of World War

II. Matters of race continued to hamper the effort, and native Hawaiians themselves were reluctant because of the growing Japanese population. Nevertheless, when the Hawaii Admissions Act was submitted to the voters of Hawaii, 93% of Hawaiians voted in favor of statehood, and Hawaii formally joined the Union on August 21, 1959. (Alaska became a state on January 3, 1959, making Hawaii the most recent of the United States.)

One small side effect of Hawaiian statehood was the change in spelling from Hawai'i to Hawaii. In the native island language, the apostrophe in Hawai'i (known as an 'okina) represented a glottal stop, which sounds like the hyphen in "uh-oh!" The Hawaiian Admissions Act dropped the 'okina, and Hawaii became the official state name. However, the University of Hawai'i and other local institutions continue to use it.

The Hawaiian Island chain consists of hundreds of islands, although only eight are considered "main islands." The largest is the island of Hawai'i (with the 'okina), often called the Big Island to avoid confusion. Although Oahu is only the third-largest of the islands, it is by far the most populous because it has the two best harbors, as previously noted. Honolulu, the state capital, is also the largest city. In 2012, the islands had a population of about 1.4 million people. The largest industry in Hawaii, unsurprisingly, is tourism, but sugarcane and pineapple are still major crops. Because of Hawaii's continued strategic importance, it is also home to a large military contingent, with Pearl Harbor and Schofield Barracks the two best known installations.

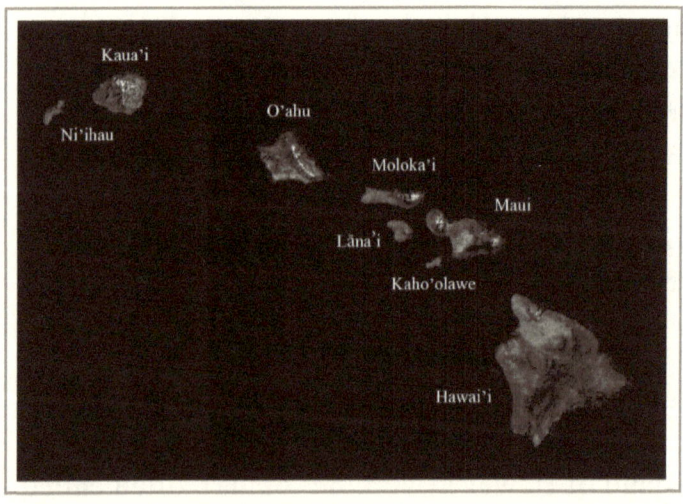

Main islands of Hawaii with labels

March 18 Holidays and Celebrations

Aniversario de la Expropiación Petrolera (Mexico)

March 18 in Mexico is a civic *fiestas patrias* (patriotic holiday) commemorating the Mexican oil expropriation of March 18, 1938, in which Mexican President Lázaro Cárdenas del Río declared that all mineral and oil reserved found within the country belonged to the nation as a whole. This resulted in an international boycott by allies of the foreign-owned companies that had run the Mexican oil market, but in spite of opposition, the new Mexican-owned Petróleos Mexicanos (PEMEX) developed into the world's fifth largest oil exporter.

Flag Day (Aruba)

On March 18, 1948, Arubans first petitioned the Netherlands for independence, and on March 18, 1986, Aruba became an autonomous state within the Kingdom of the Netherlands. Carnivals and fairs each March 18 celebrate the Aruban flag.

Flag of Aruba

Gallipoli Memorial Day (Turkey)

In Turkey, it's called *Çanakkale Savaşı,* or the Battle of Çanakkale. In English, it goes by the name of the Dardanelles Campaign or the Gallipoli Campaign of World War I, lasting from April 1915 to January 1916.

During the First World War, the British and French wanted to capture Constantinople (Istanbul), the capital of the Ottoman Empire (Turkey) in order to have a secure sea route to Russia. The campaign was a disaster for the Allies and a great victory for the Turks. It opened the way for the Turkish War of Independence and the foundation of the Republic of Turkey.

The first major Turkish victory was at sea in the Battle of March 18, in which the Turkish forces sank three battleships with only minimum casualties. That day is commemorated in Turkey as Gallipoli Memorial Day.

Men's and Soldier's Day (Mongolia)

Ten days after International Women's Day (March 8), the nation of Mongolia celebrates the establishment of its armed forces. Originally Soldier's Day, the holiday was extended to honor all men.

Christian Feast Days

Saints commemorated on March 18 include Alexander of Jerusalem, Cyril of Jerusalem, Edward the Martyr, Fridianus, and Salvator.

What Happened on March 18?

The abbreviation "O.S." on some dates refers to the fact that the Russian Empire did not switch from the Julian to the Gregorian calendar at the same time as the rest of Europe, and therefore some figures have two dates for their birth or death.

People whose original names are not in the Western alphabet have their native names in the appropriate script shown in parenthesis.

37 CE – Caligula Becomes Emperor of Rome

Tiberius, the second emperor of Rome, died March 16, 37 CE, leaving a will that named two heirs: his twelve-year old grandson Tiberius Gemellus and his 25-year old nephew Caligula. Caligula quickly consolidated power, had the Senate annul the will, and became sole emperor on March 18. Within a year, Caligula had Gemellus executed, and went on to a brief but infamous reign that ended in 41 CE, when he was assassinated by his own Praetorian Guard.

1314 CE – Jacques de Molay is Burned at the Stake

The Knights Templar started as an elite Christian military order during the Crusades but subsequently built a huge financial empire. After the end of the Crusades, tensions between the Knights and European royalty escalated.

At the urging of the French king, Pope Clement V (who lived in Avignon, France, not Rome) ordered the arrest of Jacques de Molay, Grand Master of the Knights Templar, along with many other Templars. Their assets were confiscated and a number were burned at the stake.

Although de Molay proclaimed his innocence, he, too, was convicted, and on March 18, 1314, was burned at the stake. The Knights Templar were officially disbanded.

The legend of the secretive Knights Templar is widespread in popular culture. Freemasons use some Templar symbols and rituals, especially in the Order of the Temple, but many other stories of the mysterious Templars surviving into the present day are myths.

Jacques de Molay

1741 CE – The New York Conspiracy

On March 18, 1741, a mysterious fire broke out at Fort George in lower Manhattan in what was then the British colony of New York.

A 16-year old indentured servant named Mary Burton, under threat of jail, testified that the Fort George fire and other suspicious fires were part of a conspiracy between her master, tavern owner John Hughson, and black slaves to burn down New York.

This quickly grew into a belief that a massive slave rebellion was taking place. Massive arrests put half the city's male slaves in jail. Seventeen blacks and four whites were hanged, thirteen blacks were burned at the stake, and numerous prisoners were deported.

Historians are divided about whether an actual slave plot existed at all, but are united in the belief that many who were charged and executed were not guilty.

1793 CE – First Republic in Germany

The little-known Republic of Mainz, established on March 18, 1793, in French-controlled Germany following the French

Revolution, was the first democratic state in German history, with the first elected parliament.

The republic was short-lived; Prussian troops retook the French-occupied territory, conquering Mainz on July 22 of the same year.

1834 CE – **Tolpuddle Martyrs Convicted**

Six farm laborers from Tolpuddle, a town in Dorset, England, attempted to form an early trade union, were arrested for the crime of swearing an oath to each other, convicted, and sentenced to seven years' transportation to the penal colony of Australia.

Their supporters collected 800,000 signatures for their release, organized marches and other demonstrations, and by 1837 all had returned home to England. This was an early victory for trade unionism in England.

A Tolpuddle Martyrs Museum and the annual Tolpuddle Martyrs Festival in Dorset commemorate the case.

1850 CE – Founding of American Express

On March 18, 1850, Henry Wells, William G. Fargo, and John W. Butterfield merged their express mail business into a new company called American Express, providing express shipments throughout New York state. When Butterfield objected to expanding the business westward, Wells and Fargo created another company: Wells Fargo & Co.. Under later management, the company began offering money orders and travelers cheques.

1871 CE – Paris Commune Established

On March 18, 1871, the Fourth French Revolution established the Paris Commune, a new government based on social democratic principles, including debt relief and the separation of church and state. The Commune lasted only a few months, until French forces took control of the city and deposed the government on May 28 of the same year, executing 30,000 in a massive wave of reprisals. Nevertheless, the Paris Commune became an important symbol for leftist leaders, including socialists, anarchists, and communists.

1892 CE – Stanley Cup First Awarded

Lord Stanley of Preston, 16th Earl of Derby, was appointed as Governor General of Canada in 1888. It was in Canada that he and his family were first exposed to the game of ice hockey, and became fans. Derby's sons played in amateur leagues in Ottawa, and in 1892 donated a challenge cup to be awarded to the best amateur hockey team in Canada. In 1909, the Stanley Cup began to be awarded to professional teams only, and is the championship trophy given to the National Hockey League (NHL) playoff winner each year.

Original Stanley Cup

1931 CE – George I of Greece Assassinated

Danish Prince William of Schleswig-Holstein-Sonderburg-Glücksberg was elected King of the Hellenes (Greece) by the Greek National Assembly at the age of 17.

He married Russian Grand Duchess Olga Constantinova and they had eight children. (His son Andrew was the father of Prince Philip, consort of Queen Elizabeth II.)

He reigned for nearly 50 years, but while walking through the streets of Thessaloniki without bodyguards, he was shot in the back by Alexandros Schinas, an alcoholic vagrant who killed the King because "he refused to give me money."

1921 CE – **Peace of Riga**

The Peace of Riga ended the three-year Soviet-Polish War, ceding large parts of Ukraine and Belarus to Poland. The new borders of Poland would exist until World War II.

1922 CE – **Gandhi Jailed**

As a result of the "non-cooperation" movement, Mohandas Gandhi was arrested by the British for sedition, convicted and sentenced to six years. He began his sentence on March 18, 1922, but would be released in only two years for an appendicitis operation.

1925 CE – **Tri-State Tornado**

The deadliest tornado in U.S. history traveled 219 miles, the longest distance ever recorded, on Wednesday, March 18, 1925. Beginning in southeastern Missouri, it traveled through southern Illinois and into southwestern Indiana, killing 695 people and injuring over 2,000 more. The total damage of $16.5 million translates into the equivalent of over $2 billion in 2012.

1937 CE – New London School Explosion

A natural gas leak triggered an explosion on March 18, 1937, destroying a school in New London, Texas. It killed more than 295 students and teachers in the deadliest school disaster in American history.

1937 CE – Human-Powered Flight Record

On March 18, 1937, the *Pedaliante,* a human-powered airplane designed by Enea Bossi and piloted by bicyclist Emilio Casco, was launched by catapult to a height of 9 meters (30 feet). Casco successfully pedaled the plane to fly 1 km, setting a world record for human-powered flight.

1942 CE – War Relocation Authority Established

The War Relocation Authority, established by executive order on March 18, 1942, was responsible for the forced relocation and detention of Japanese, German, and Italian American citizens during World War II.

Japanese family awaiting relocation

1944 CE – **Mount Vesuvius Erupts**

The Italian volcano Mount Vesuvius erupted on March 14, 1944, destroying four Italian villages and over 75 aircraft of the U.S. Army Air Force 340th Bombardment Group stationed in Italy during World War II.

1965 CE – **First Space Walk**

On March 18, 1965, cosmonaut Alexey Leonov (Алексе́й Лео́нов), one of the two crewmembers aboard Voskhod 2 (Восход-2) left his spacecraft for a 12 minute, 9 second walk in space, the first time a human being had done so.

Voskhod 2 Mission Patch

1969 CE – Operation Menu

During the Vietnam War, the U.S. conducted a secret bombing campaign against North Vietnam bases in Cambodia and Laos, beginning on March 18, 1969 and lasting until May 1970. The details of the bombing campaign were declassified in 2000.

1974 CE – End of the Oil Embargo

In October 1973, the Organization of Arab Petroleum Exporting Companies (OAPEC) proclaimed an oil embargo against the United States for its aid to Israel during the Yom Kippur War. Crude oil prices in the U.S. quadrupled and gas lines became common. The U.S. negotiated an Israeli pullback from the Sinai and Golan Heights as the Arabs withdrew from Israeli territory, and the embargo was officially lifted on March 18, 1974.

1990 CE – Largest Art Theft in History

Two thieves disguised as Boston police officers entered Boston's Isabella Stewart Gardner Museum early on the morning of March 18, 1990. They stole 13 pieces, including paintings by Vermeer, Rembrandt, Degas, and Manet, as well as other artifacts worth an estimated $500 million, making the robbery the largest private property theft in history. To date, the stolen art has not yet been returned, and a reward of $5 million has not been claimed.

Rembrandt's *The Storm on the Sea of Galilee*, one of the stolen paintings

Who Was Born on March 18?

Acting and Film

Madeline Carroll (March 18, 1996 —)

Carroll appeared as Molly in 2008's *Swing Vote* and co-starred in 2010's *Flipped*.

Lily Collins (March 18, 1989 —)

Collins appeared in the films *The Blind Side, Abduction*, and *Mirror, Mirror*.

Adam Pally (March 18, 1982 —)

Pally is best known as Max Blum in the ABC sitcom *Happy Endings*.

Danneel Harris (March 18, 1979 —)

Harris is known for playing Shannon McBain on *One Life to Live* and Rachel Gatina on *One Tree Hill*.

Sutton Foster (March 18, 1975 —)

Foster won two Tony Awards for her Broadway appearances in *Thoroughly Modern Millie* and *Anything Goes*, and stars in the ABC Family series *Bunheads*.

Vanessa L. Williams (March 18, 1963 —)

Vanessa Williams was the first African-American named Miss America, but was forced to relinquish her title when Penthouse magazine published nude photographs of her taken earlier. Her hit "Save the Best for Last" reached #1 on the pop charts and "Colors of the Wind" from the Disney feature *Pocahontas* reached #4. She was Wilhelmina in the sitcom *Ugly Betty* and Renee in *Desperate Housewives*.

Vanessa Williams

Mike Rowe (March 18, 1962 —)

Rowe is known as the host of the Discovery Channel series *Dirty Jobs*.

Richard Biggs (March 18, 1960 — May 22, 2004)

Biggs played Dr. Marcus Hunter on *Days of Our Lives* and Dr. Stephen Franklin on *Babylon 5*.

Luc Besson (March 18, 1959 —)

French auteur Luc Besson is known for such films as *The Fifth Element* and *La Femme Nikita*.

Brad Dourif (March 18, 1950 —)

Dourif's first major role was Billy in *One Flew Over the Cuckoo's Nest*. He was the voice of Chucky in the *Child's Play* franchise and played Gríma Wormtongue in *The Lord of the Rings* films.

Kevin Dobson (March 18, 1943 —)

Kevin Dobson played Detective Crocker on *Kojak*, Mac McKenzie on *Knots Landing*, and Mickey Horton on *Days of Our Lives*.

John Mollo (March 18, 1931 —)

Costume designer John Mollo won two Academy Awards for his work on the first *Star Wars* film and for 1983's *Gandhi*.

Peter Graves (March 18, 1926 — March 14, 2010)

Peter Graves was best known for his starring role in the television series *Mission: Impossible*. He was the younger brother of actor James Arness.

Peter Graves (right) and the *Mission: Impossible* 5th season cast

René Clément (March 18, 1913 — March 17, 1996)

Director René Clément won two Academy Awards for Best Foreign Language Film for 1950's *Au-delà des grilles* and 1952's *Jeux interdits*.

Smiley Burnette (March 18, 1911 — February 16, 1967)

Actor and country music performer Lester Burnett was known as Gene Autry's sidekick and for his role in the sitcom Petticoat Junction. He could play over 100 musical instruments, and composed such songs as "Ridin' Down the Canyon (To Watch the Sun Go Down)" and "On the Strings of My Lonesome Guitar." He also invented one of the first home audiovisual systems, "Cinevision Talkies."

Robert Donat (March 18, 1905 — June 9, 1958)

Donat won the Academy Award for Best Actor for *Goodbye Mr. Chips* and also appeared in Alfred Hitchcock's *The 39 Steps*.

Edward Everett Horton (March 18, 1886 — September 29, 1970)

Character actor Edward Everett Horton is primarily known for his work in the Fred Astaire/Ginger Rogers films, in which he often played Astaire's sidekick. Later, he narrated the "Fractured Fairy Tales" cartoons for *The Rocky and Bullwinkle Show*.

Edward Everett Horton

Arts and Literature

Will Durst (March 18, 1952 —)

Satirist Will Durst was a contributing editor of *National Lampoon* and covered the 1992 political conventions for the Comedy Channel.

Joy Fielding (March 18, 1945 —)

Fielding is known for *See Jane Run*, adapted into a movie, and *Kiss Mommy Goodbye*.

John Updike (March 18, 1932 — January 27, 2009)

Novelist John Updike's most famous work is his series of novels about Harry "Rabbit" Angstrom, beginning with 1960's *Rabbit, Run*. Two of the novels in that series won the Pulitzer Prize.

George Plimpton (March 18, 1927 — September 25, 2003)

Journalist, sportswriter, and editor George Plimpton was a founder of *The Paris Review*, helped wrestle Sirhan Sirhan to the ground after he shot and killed Presidential candidate Robert Kennedy, wrote *Paper Lion* about his preseason training with the Detroit Lions, and appeared in a number of films including *The Bonfire of the Vanities* and *Good Will Hunting*.

Bob Broeg (March 18, 1918 — October 28, 2005)

Sportswriter Bob Broeg coined the nickname "Stan the Man" for Stan Musial. He was on the board of the Baseball Hall of Fame and was elected to the National Sportscasters and Sportswriters Hall of Fame in 1997.

Richard Condon (March 18, 1915 — April 9, 1996)

Condon is best known for his 1959 novel *The Manchurian Candidate* and for his novels about a gangster family, including *Prizzi's Honor.*

William Johnson (March 18, 1901 — January 1, 1970)

Harlem Renaissance artist William Johnson's work *(next page)* in realistic, expressionistic, and folk styles was given a major exhibition by the Smithsonian American Art Museum.

Wilfred Owen (March 18, 1893 — November 4, 1918)

Soldier Wilfred Owen became one of the leading British poets of World War I, writing about the horrors of trench warfare and poison gas. His famous poems include "Dulce et Decorum Est" and "Anthem for Doomed Youth." He was killed in action one week before the armistice.

"Street Musicians" by William Johnson, 1939-1940

Stéphane Mallarmé (March 18, 1842 — September 9, 1898)

French symbolist poet Stéphane Mallarmé inspired the development of such artistic schools as Dadaism, Surrealism, and Futurism. His poem The *Afternoon of a Faun (L'après-midi d'un faune)* inspired Claude Debussy's composition *Prélude à l'après-midi d'un faune* and the ballet *Afternoon of the Faun* choreographed by Vaslav Nijinsky, which was both controversial in its day and highly influential in the development of modern dance.

Madame de La Fayette (baptized March 18, 1634 — May 25, 1693)

Madame de La Fayette wrote *La Princesse de Clèves,* one of the earliest novels in literature. The book was hugely popular in its day and continues to be regarded as a classic. Five films and a radio play have been based on the book.

The book became newsworthy in 2006 when French president Nicolas Sarkozy made negative comments about the book's use in civil service exams, resulting in public outcry and a surge in sales.

Business

Peter Jones (March 18, 1966 —)

British entrepreneur Peter Jones's businesses include mobile phones, television, media, leisure, and real estate. He is known for his appearances on the BBC Two show *Dragon's Den* and the American TV show *American Inventor*.

Ben Cohen (March 18, 1951 —)

Cohen co-founded Ben & Jerry's ice cream.

Dick Smith (March 18, 1944 —)

Australian businessman Dick Smith founded Dick Smith Electronics, Dick Smith Foods, and Australian Geographic, but is better known for the first solo helicopter flight around the world, flying over Mount Everest, attempting to tow an iceberg from Antarctica to Australia, and serving as conductor aboard a London double-decker bus that jumped 15 motorcycles.

Andy Granatelli (March 18, 1923 —)

Auto mechanic and racing promoter Granatelli was CEO and spokesman of STP motor oil company. He is a member of the International Motorsports Hall of Fame, the Motorsports Hall of Fame of America and the National Sprint Car Hall of Fame.

Ernest Gallo (March 18, 1909 — March 6, 2007)

Gallo co-founded E & J Gallo Winery with his brother Julio, beginning with $5,900 in borrowed money. Both brothers became billionaires.

Jacob Bunn (March 18, 1814 or 1800 — October 16, 1897)

The Bunn brothers, Jacob and John Whitfield Bunn, were personal friends of Abraham Lincoln, assisting in his political campaigns, and built a huge business empire consisting of railroads, banks, stock exchanges, manufacturing companies, grocery stores, and others. They were a major force in the economic and political development of the American Midwest.

Engineering and Science

Jake Swirbul (March 18, 1889 — June 28, 1960)

Aviation pioneer Jake Swirbul co-founded Grumman Aircraft.

Rudolf Diesel (March 18, 1858 — September 29, 1913)

German engineer Rudolf Diesel invented the Diesel engine. He died mysteriously while crossing the English channel, vanishing from aboard a steamship. A corpse with his personal items was found ten days later, but the circumstances of his death were never confirmed.

He left a bag for his wife Martha with 200,000 German marks in cash along with financial statements that revealed their bank accounts were virtually empty.

The Rudolf-Diesel-Medaille is awarded by the German Institute for Inventions in his honor.

Nathanael Green Herreshoff (March 18, 1848 — June 2, 1938)

Yacht designer Herreshoff was known as the "Wizard of Bristol" for his revolutionary designs *(next page)* that produced five America's Cup winners, the first U.S. Navy torpedo boats, and created a number of technical innovations in ship design.

The Herreshoff Marine Museum in Bristol, Rhode Island, preserves his many achievements. Some of his yachts continue to be raced today.

The 1903 America's Cup defender *Reliance*, designed by
Nathanael Herreshoff

Christian Goldbach (March 18, 1690 — November 20, 1764)

German mathematician Christian Goldbach developed Goldbach's conjecture, one of the oldest still-unsolved problems in number theory, which states that every even integer greater than 2 can be expressed as the sum of two primes. Although this is known to be true for every number from 3 to 4,000,000,000,000,000,000 (10^{18}), there is still no proof that it is true for all numbers. He is also known for two theorems, the Goldbach-Euler theorem and Goldbach's theorem.

Music

Adam Levine (March 18, 1979 —)

Levine was front man and guitarist for the pop rock band Maroon 5 and was a coach on the American talent show *The Voice*.

Queen Latifah (March 18, 1970 —)

Dana Elaine Owens is a singer, rapper, and actress who was won a Golden Globe, two Screen Actor Guild Awards, two Image Awards, and a Grammy. She gained mainstream success as the matron in the film adaptation of *Chicago*.

Jerry Cantrell (March 18, 1966 —)

Cantrell was lead guitarist, co-lead vocalist, and main songwriter for Alice in Chains.

Irene Cara (March 18, 1959 —)

Cara received a Golden Globe nomination for her role in the 1980 film *Fame*, and had an hit with the song "Fame" from the film. She won an Academy Award and a Golden Globe Award for Best Original Song for co-writing "Flashdance... What a Feeling." She was first African-American woman to win a Golden Globe.

John Hartman (March 18, 1950 —)

Hartman was co-founder and original drummer of the Doobie Brothers.

B. J. Wilson (March 18, 1947 — October 8, 1990)

Wilson was the drummer for Procul Harum and was the drummer on the film soundtrack of *The Rocky Horror Picture Show*.

Dennis Linde (March 18, 1943 — December 22, 2006)

Dennis Linde is best known as the writer of the 1972 Elvis Presley hit "Burning Love." He wrote songs for Roger Miller, the Dixie Chicks, and Tanya Tucker. He was inducted into the Nashville Songwriters Hall of Fame in 2001.

Wilson Pickett (March 18, 1941 — January 19, 2006)

R&B singer and songwriter Wilson Pickett is best known for his hits "In the Midnight Hour," "Land of 1,000 Dances," and "Mustang Sally." He was inducted into the Rock and Roll Hall of Fame in 1991.

Charley Pride (March 18, 1938 —)

Country music singer Charley Pride (below) was the best-selling artist for RCA Records since Elvis Presley and was the second African-American member of the Grand Ole Opry. His hits include "Just Between You and Me" and "Kiss an Angel Good Mornin'."

John Kander (March 18, 1927 —)

As part of the songwriting team of Kander and Ebb, John Kander composed such musicals as *Cabaret, Chicago*, and *Kiss of the Spider Woman*, and composed scores for films including *Kramer vs. Kramer* and *Billy Bathgate*.

Jean Goldkette (March 18, 1893 — March 24, 1962)

Critics say that influential early jazz bandleader Jean Goldkette's innovative arrangements made his band "the first original white swing band in jazz history." Musicians including Bix Beiderbecke, Hoagy Carmichael, Tommy Dorsey, and many others played in Goldkette's bands.

Nikolai Rimsky-Korsakov (Николай Ри́мский-Ко́рсаков) (March 18 [O.S. March 6], 1844 — June 21 [O.S. June 8], 1908)

Russian composer Rimsky-Korsakov was an extremely influential figure in the development of modern classical music. His orchestral compositions, including *Capriccio Espangnol*, the *Russian Easter Festival Overture*, and *Scherezade* are part of the classical repertoire, but he is most famous to Western audiences for "The Flight of the Bumblebee" from his opera *The Tale of Tsar Saltan*.

Nikolai Rimsky-Korsakov

Newsmakers

Christer Fuglesang (March 18, 1957 —)

In 2006, physicist Fuglesang became the first Swedish citizen in space on the STS-116 Space Shuttle mission. He participated in two missions and five spacewalks.

Deborah Jean Palfrey (March 18, 1956 — May 1, 2008)

Known as the "D.C. Madam," Palfrey was convicted of racketeering and money laundering as the operator of an escort agency in Washington, DC. She hanged herself after being sentenced to prison.

Michael Reagan (March 18, 1945 —)

Syndicated radio host Michael Reagan is the adopted son of Ronald Reagan and his first wife Jane Wyman.

Frank Searle (March 18, 1921 — March 26, 2005)

Loch Ness Monster researcher Frank Searle became known for his photographs of the monster that turned out to be fakes. His story was told in the documentary *The Man Who Captured Nessie.*

Werner Mölders (March 18, 1913 — November 22, 1941)

Luftwaffe pilot Werner Mölders (right) was the leading German fighter ace in the Spanish Civil War and the first pilot in history to claim 100 aerial victories. He fought on the Eastern Front in World War II, and invented new fighter tactics.

Edgar Cayce (March 18, 1877 — January 3, 1945)

Famous psychic Edgar Cayce claimed to be able to answer questions on health, past lives, business, dream interpretation, and other topics while in a trance state. His clients included such luminaries as Woodrow Wilson, Thomas Edison, Irving Berlin, and George Gershwin.

Emilie Kempin-Spyri (March 18, 1853 — April 12, 1901)

Niece of *Heidi* author Johanna Spyri, Kempin-Spyri was the first woman in Europe to earn a Doctor of Law degree. Forbidden to practice in Switzerland, she established the first women's law college in New York and continued to fight to be admitted to practice in her home country. The law finally changed in 1898.

Politics

F. W. de Klerk (March 18, 1936 —)

F. W. de Klerk was the last president of apartheid-era South Africa. He won the 1993 Nobel Peace Prize, shared with Nelson Mandela.

Fidel Ramos (March 18, 1928 —)

Fidel Ramos was president of the Philippines from 1992 to 1998.

Fred Shuttlesworth (March 18, 1922 — October 5, 2011)

Birmingham, Alabama, pastor and civil rights activist Fred Shuttlesworth co-founded the Southern Christian Leadership Conference. The Birmingham-Shuttlesworth International Airport (BHM) is named in his honor.

Neville Chamberlain (March 18, 1869 — November 9, 1940)

British Conservative Prime Minister Neville Chamberlain is best known for a foreign policy of appeasement, leading to his signing of the 1938 Munich Agreement that gave the Sudentenland region of Czechoslovakia to Adolf Hitler's Germany on Hitler's promise that he would take no further aggressive actions.

His famous speech, "I have returned from Germany with peace in our time" turned out to be false, and Chamberlain led the British government during the first eight months of World War II, until he was succeeded by Winston Churchill.

William Sulzer (March 18, 1863 — November 6, 1941)

Reformer William "Plain Bill" Sulzer was the first and so far only New York governor to be impeached on charges of perjury and fraud. He began his career as part of the Tammany Hall machine but turned against it. The 1940 Preston Sturges film, *The Great McGinty*, is partially based on Sulzer's story.

Grover Cleveland (March 18, 1837 — June 24, 1908)

Grover Cleveland was the 22nd and 24th President of the United States, the only president to have served two non-consecutive terms. He won the popular vote to be the 23rd president, but lost in the Electoral College, the third time in U.S. history that a presidential candidate won the popular vote but lost the election.

Cleveland was accused of having fathered an illegitimate child, leading to the anti-Cleveland slogan, "Ma, Ma, where's my Pa?" to which Cleveland's supporters replied, "Gone to the White House, Ha! Ha! Ha!"

Anti-Cleveland political cartoon from 1884 by Frank Beard

Francis Lieber (March 18, 1798 or 1800 — October 2, 1972)

German-born South Carolina jurist and philosopher developed the Lieber Code (*Code for the Government of Armies in the Field*) during the American Civil War, which was the basis for the first laws of war.

He also edited the Encyclopaedia Americana, founded the first swimming school in America, and was in charge of preserving the records of the Confederate government after the Civil War.

The year of his birth is uncertain because he lied about his age to serve in the Prussian Army during the Napoleonic Wars. He was wounded at the Battle of Waterloo and fought in the Greek War of Independence before moving to the U.S..

John C. Calhoun (March 18, 1782 — March 31, 1850)

South Carolina politician John C. Calhoun was Vice President under both John Quincy Adams and Andrew Jackson, served as Secretary of State and War, and was both a senator and representative from South Carolina.

He is best remembered today for his active defense of slavery as a "positive good," and is considered a force in the eventual secession of the American South that led to the Civil War.

Daguerreotype of John C. Calhoun by Matthew Brady

Miloš Obrenović I, Prince of Serbia (Милош Обреновић) (March 18 [O.S. March 7], 1780 — September 26, 1860)

Prince Obrenović led Serbian forces in the Second Serbian Uprising that made Serbia an autonomous duchy in the Ottoman Empire and started the process of reëstablishing Serbian statehood and shaping the policies of the modern Serbian state.

Sports

Rebecca Soni (March 18, 1987 —)

Swimmer Soni won six Olympic medals, set world records in the 100-meter and 200-meter breaststrokes, and received the American Swimmer of the Year Award for three consecutive years.

Tora Berger (March 18, 1981 —)

Norwegian biathlete Berger won a gold medal in the 2010 Winter Olympics and four gold, three silver, and five bronze medals in World Championship games.

Alexei Yagudin (Алексей Константинович Ягудин) (March 18, 1980 —)

Russian figure skater Yagudin won a gold medal at the 2002 Winter Olympics. He won the World Championship four times and the European Championship three times, among other achievements.

Antonio Margarito (March 18, 1978 —)

Mexican-American professional boxer Margarito won the Welterweight Championship in 2002.

Bonnie Blair (March 18, 1964 —)

Speed skater Bonnie Blair represented the United States in four Olympics, winning five gold and one bronze medal.

Ingemar Stenmark (March 18, 1956 —)

Alpine skier Stenmark won two gold medals in slalom at the 1980 Winter Olympics.

Rick Martel (March 18, 1956 —)

WWF wrestler Rick Martel won numerous championships in his 15 year professional career.

Mike Webster (March 18, 1952 — September 24, 2002)

NFL center "Iron Mike" Webster played with the Pittsburgh Steelers and the Kansas City Chiefs and was elected to the Pro Football Hall of Fame. He died of chronic traumatic encephalopathy, suffering amnesia, dementia, and depression in the years before his death at the age of 50.

Rod Milburn (March 18, 1950 — November 11, 1997)

American athlete Ron Milburn won a gold medal in the 110m hurdles in the 1972 Summer Olympics and tied the world record three times.

He died when he fell into a tank of sodium chlorate solution while working in a Louisiana paper plant.

Alex Higgins (March 18, 1949 — July 24, 2010)

"Hurricane" Higgins won the Snooker World Championship twice, was World Doubles Champion, and won the World Cup three times with the All Ireland team.

Guy Lapointe (March 18, 1948 —)

NHL star Guy Lapointe was elected to the Hockey Hall of Fame in 1993.

Ron Atkinson (March 18, 1939 —)

Former soccer player and manager "Big Ron" Atkinson is best known for his idiosyncratic "Ronglish" turns of phrase, and for his controversial comments on race and gender.

Mark Donohue (March 18, 1937 — August 19, 1975)

Nicknamed both "Captain Nice" and "Dark Monohue," racecar driver Mark Donahue won the 1972 Indianapolis 500 and racked up multiple NASCAR and Formula One wins.

He wrote *The Unfair Advantage* about his racing career, and is a member of the International Motorsports Hall of Fame and the Sports Car Club of America Hall of Fame.

Dick Littlefield (March 18, 1926 — November 20, 1997)

Pitcher Littlefield of the New York Giants is known for being traded (along with $30,000, equivalent to $250,000 in 2012) for Jackie Robinson of the Dodgers. Robinson retired instead, and the trade was voided.

Constante Girardengo (March 18, 1893 — February 9, 1978)

Bicycle racer Girardengo was considered one of the finest riders in the history of the sport, declared *campionissimo* ("champion of champions") by his adoring fans.

He was considered to be more popular than Mussolini in his day, so much so that the government decreed that all express trains should stop in his home town, an honor previously given only to heads of state.

He was ranked #1 in the world from 1919 to 1926.

Who Died on March 18?

Acting and Film

Fess Parker (August 16, 1924 — March 18, 2010)

Fess Parker (right) is best known for playing Davy Crockett in the Walt Disney TV miniseries and Daniel Boone in the TV series of the same name. Following his acting career, he operated the Fess Parker Winery.

Natasha Richardson (May 11, 1963 — March 18, 2009)

A member of the Redgrave acting dynasty, Richardson won a Tony for her performance in the 1998 revival of *Cabaret* and appeared in such films as *The Handmaid's Tale, The Parent Trap,* and *Maid in Manhattan.* She died in a skiing accident in 2009.

Anthony Minghella (January 6, 1954 — March 18, 2008)

Minghella won the Academy Award for Best Director for the 1996 movie *The English Patient.*

Michael Atwell (January 16, 1943 — March 18, 2006)

Atwell is best known as Kenny Beale from the British soap opera *EastEnders.*

Robin Harris (August 30, 1953 — March 18, 1990)

Harris appeared in movies including *I'm Gonna Git You Sucka, Do The Right Thing,* and *House Party.* He was best known for his comic sketch *Bébé's Kids.*

Barbara Bates (August 6, 1925 — March 18, 1969)

Bates played Phoebe in 1950's *All About Eve.*

Wanda Hawley (July 30, 1895 — March 18, 1963)

Silent screen star Wanda Hawley co-starred with Rudolph Valentino in *The Young Rajah* and with Douglas Fairbanks in *Mr. Fix-It*. She did not survive the transition to talkies, and ended her career as a call girl in San Francisco.

Wanda Hawley on the cover of *Motion Picture Classic*, 1920

Business and Building

Adam Osborne (March 6, 1939 — March 18, 2003)

Adam Osborne built the first commercially available portable computer, the Osborne 1, which weighed 24.5 pounds but cost half what comparable desktop machines of the time sold for. He created a publishing company specializing in computer manuals, which later became Osborne/McGraw-Hill.

William C. Durant (December 8, 1861 — March 18, 1947)

Automotive pioneer Durant co-founded General Motors and Chevrolet.

Henry Janeway Hardenbergh (February 6, 1847 — March 18, 1918)

Among Hardenbergh's famous buildings are the original Waldorf-Astoria and the Dakota Building (next page), best known as the home of John Lennon, Lauren Bacall, Leonard Bernstein, Judy Garland, Boris Karloff, and many others.

Henry Janeway Hardenbergh's Dakota Apartments, 1880s.

Exploration and Nature

Dan Gibson (January 19, 1922 — March 18, 2006)

Photographer and sound recordist Gibson made nature films for the 78-episode TV series *Audubon Wildlife Theatre* and invented the Dan Gibson Parabolic Microphone. He received the Order of Canada for his environmental work.

Prince Luigi Amedeo, Duke of the Abruzzi (January 29, 1873 — March 18, 1933)

Italian nobleman Luigi Amedeo made an attempt to reach the North Pole in 1900, coming closer than any attempt to that date. He made the second attempt to climb the mountain K2, second highest on Earth, setting a world altitude record for mountain climbing. He commanded the Adriatic fleet during World War I.

Johnny Appleseed (September 26, 1774 — March 18, 1845)

Nurseryman John Chapman became known as Johnny Appleseed for introducing apple trees to large part of Pennsylvania, Ohio, Indiana, and Illinois. He was also a missionary for the Swedenborgian church.

Music

"Papa John" Phillips (August 30, 1935 — March 18, 2001

Phillips was leader of the 1960's pop group The Mamas & the Papas (next page) and the father of actress Mackenzie Phillips and singer Chynna Phillips.

The Mamas and the Papas on the *Ed Sullivan Show*, 1968. From left to right, Michelle Phillips, Cass Elliot, Denny Doherty, and John Phillips

Politics and Public Affairs

William Christopher (October 27, 1925 — March 18, 2011)

Christopher was Secretary of State during Bill Clinton's first term.

Elizabeth Huckaby (April 14, 1905 — March 18, 1999)

Little Rock Central High School Vice-Principal for Girls Elizabeth Huckaby was responsible for protecting the first black female students admitted to the school, an event so resisted by the community that the 101st Airborne Battle Group was sent to escort them into the school.

Umberto II of Italy (May 9, 1946 — March 18, 1893)

Umberto II was the last King of Italy. His reign lasted just over a month, following a constitutional referendum in which Italy changed from a monarchy to a republic. He lived the rest of his life in exile.

Farouk I of Egypt (فاروق الأول) (February 11, 1920 — March 18, 1965)

King Farouk I of Egypt was known for his corruption and lavish lifestyle. He was overthrown in the Egyptian Revolution of 1952 and also spent the rest of his life in exile.

Eleftherios Venizelos (Ἐλευθέριος Βενιζέλος) (August 23, 1864 — March 18, 1936)

Greek revolutionary, statesman, and prime minister Venizelos is widely credited as "the maker of modern Greece."

Matilda Joslyn Gage (March 24, 1826 — March 18, 1898)

Growing up in a house that was a station on the Underground Railroad, Gage became involve in women's right and suffrage. She was president of the National Woman Suffrage Association and founded the Women's National Liberal Union. She co-authored *History of Woman Suffrage* with Elizabeth Cady Stanton and edited *The National Citizen*. She was the mother-in-law of *Wizard of Oz* creator L. Frank Baum.

Robert Walpole, 1st Earl of Oxford (August 26, 1676 — March 18, 1745)

Walpole is generally considered the first Prime Minister of Great Britain. He held the office from approximately 1721 to 1742, the longest administration in British history. He was often called "the fat old Squire of Norfolk."

John Dixwell (1607 — March 18, 1689)

One of the judges who signed the death warrant of English monarch Charles I, Dixwell had to flee the country when the Protectorate of Oliver Cromwell ended and the monarchy was restored. He settled in the colony of New Haven, Connecticut, and lived under a fake identity until his death.

Ivan the Terrible (Ива́н Васи́льевич) (August 25, 1530 — March 28 [O.S. March 18], 1584)

Grand Prince of Moscow Ivan IV Vasilyevich (right) was crowned the first Tsar of All the Russias in 1547. He conquered the lands of Kazan, Astrakhan, and Siberia, turning the small state of Moscow into a great empire.

The "Terrible" title in Russian means "inspiring fear or terror" or being formidable and dangerous.

Although intelligent and devout, he suffered from mental illness and fits of rage. During one such rage, he beat his son and heir to death.

Edward the Martyr (c. 962 — March 18, 978)

Edward, King of the English, was murdered and the throne taken by his half-brother Æthelred the Unready after only three years as monarch. After his death, he was portrayed as a martyr and canonized as a saint.

Alexander Severus (October 1, 208 — March 18 or 19, 235)

The 26th emperor of Rome, Alexander Severus ruled from 222 to 235 CE. He came to the throne on the assassination of Elagabalus and was assassinated himself seventeen years later in a conspiracy by his own legions. This ended the Severan dynasty and triggered the Crisis of the Third Century, a 50-year period of civil war, plague and economic collapse that nearly destroyed the empire.

Science and Mathematics

Marcellin Berthelot (October 25, 1827 — March 18, 1907)

Considered one of the greatest chemists of all time, Marcellin Berthelot is known for the Thomsen-Berthelot principle of thermochemistry.

Augustus De Morgan (June 27, 1806 — March 18, 1871)

Indian-born British mathematician De Morgan formulated De Morgan's laws, a system describing propositional logic. The laws are used extensively in electrical and computer engineering. He also developed De Morgan algebra, used to study fuzzy logic, a form of probabilistic logic that allows treatment of approximate and partially true values.

Sports

Jack Quinlan (January 23, 1927 — March 18, 1965)

Sportscaster Jack Quinlan was best known for his coverage of the Chicago Cubs.

Henri Cornet (August 4, 1884 — March 18, 1941)

Cyclist Henri Cornet won the 1904 Tour de France at the age of 19, the youngest winner ever.

Writing

Andrew Britton (January 6, 1981 — March 18, 2008)

Britton hit the New York Times Bestseller List with his espionage novels *The American, The Assassin,* and *The Invisible.*

R. A. Lafferty (November 7, 1914 — March 18, 2002)

Award-winning science fiction writer R. A. Lafferty was known for his quirky and original language.

Bernard Malamud (April 26, 1914 — March 18, 1986)

Malamud was considered one of the great American Jewish authors of the 20th century. His novel *The Natural* was turned into a 1984 film starring Robert Redford, and his novel *The Fixer* won both the National Book Award and the Pulitzer Prize.

Erich Fromm (March 23, 1900 — March 18, 1980)

Psychologist and philosopher Erich Fromm is known for his 1956 international bestseller *The Art of Loving* and for his 1941 work *Escape From Freedom.*

Leigh Brackett (December 7, 1915 — March 18, 1978)

As one of the few female science fiction writer in the pulp magazine era, Leigh Brackett was famous for her stories of adventure on Mars.

She found greater fame as a screenwriter, however, writing the scripts for *The Big Sleep, Rio Bravo*, and *Star Wars Episode V: The Empire Strikes Back.*

Laurence Sterne (November 24, 1713 — March 18, 1768)

Novelist and clergyman Sterne is best known for his novel *The Life and Opinions of Tristram Shandy, Gentlemen*, or *Tristram Shandy* for short.

March: The Third Month

Up from the sea, the wild north wind is blowing
Under the sky's gray arch;
Smiling I watch the shaken elm boughs, knowing
It is the wind of March.

— "March," John Greenleaf Whittier

In ancient Rome, March was the first month of the year. As the first month of spring, in the Mediterranean climate it marked the beginning of the military campaign season. That's why March (Martius) is named in honor of Mars, the Roman god of war.

Although the first month of the year was moved back to January sometime during the transition of Rome from a kingdom to a republic (historians differ), March was the first month of the year in Russia until the end of the 15th Century, and is the first month of the year in many other cultures and religions.

In the northern hemisphere, March 1 marks the beginning of meteorological spring. In the southern hemisphere, March is the equivalent of September, making southern hemisphere March the beginning of autumn.

March is one of the seven months that have 31 days in it. March starts on the same day of the week as November every year, and except for leap years starts on the same day as February. March starts on the same day of the week as the previous June except for leap years, and in leap years starts on the same day as the previous September and December.

March in Other Cultures

In Finland, March is called *maaliskuu* (earthy month). In Ukraine, it's *березень* (birch tree). Other names for March include *Lentmonat* (Saxon), *Hyld-monath* (Angles), and *sušec* (Slovene).

March Symbols

Birthstones: Aquamarine and bloodstone, both representing courage.

Aquamarine

Birth Flowers: Daffodils

Daffodils in Bagatelle Park, Paris, France

March Events

Honorary months: Presidents, Congresses, and nations around the world issue proclamations recognizing particular months to honor certain causes. These events generally fall in March. (All US unless otherwise noted.)

- National Nutrition Month
- American Red Cross Month
- Women's History Month (celebrated in Canada during October)

- Irish-American Heritage Month
- Colorectal Cancer Awareness Month
- Fire Prevention Month (The Philippines)

"March Madness": (United States) The NCAA Men's Division I Basketball Championship, popularly known as "March Madness" or the "Big Dance," is a single-elimination tournament to establish the champion college basketball team.

Multi-day events: Some March events span multiple days.

- **Nineteen Day Fast:** (Bahá'í Faith) March 2 through March 20

- **Girl Scout Week:** (U.S.) The week that includes March 12, the date of the founding of the first chapter of the Girl Scouts of the USA in 1912. The earliest Girl Scout Week can start is March 6, and the latest it can end is March 18. The Sunday of Girl Scout Week is celebrated by some churches as Girl Scout Sunday or Girl Scout Sabbath.

- **Multiple Sclerosis Awareness Week:** (U.S.) Sponsored by the National Multiple Sclerosis Society, MS Awareness Week is normally held on the second full week in March. The earliest it can begin is March 9 and the latest it can end is March 21.

Movable events: Some events change dates from year to year.

- **Passion Sunday:** The fifth Sunday of the Christian season of Lent is known as Passion Sunday in various Protestant denominations and by some traditionalist Catholics. Sometimes, the sixth Sunday of Lent is referred to as Passion Sunday, but it is more commonly known as Palm Sunday. Passion Sunday starts the two week Passiontide, which ends on Holy Saturday, the day before Easter, commemorating the day that Jesus's body was laid in the tomb. The fifth Sunday of Lent can occur as early as March 8 (though the next time it will be that early is in 2285 CE), and as late as April 11.

- **Palm Sunday:** The moveable feast of Palm Sunday commemorates the triumphant entry of Jesus into Jerusalem, an event mentioned in all four gospels. In many Christian churches, palm leaves are distributed to the worshippers. The earliest date for Palm Sunday is March 15, and the latest is April 18.

The month of March, from the illuminated manuscript *Les Très Riches Heures du duc de Berry*

March Zodiac Signs

From the perspective of someone on Earth, the Sun appears to move through the sky throughout the year, along a path astronomers call the ecliptic plane. The ecliptic plane is divided into twelve constellations, known as the zodiac, based on traditionally observed patterns of stars. On your birthday, you can't see your constellation, because it's part of the daytime sky.

The zodiac was first developed by Babylonian astronomers about 2,500 years ago. Because they were unaware that the Earth wobbles like a spinning top (a motion known as *precession*), they didn't make allowance for the fact that the Sun's path through the zodiac changes over time.

That means there are now two sets of dates for your birth sign. The tropical dates are the original Babylonian dates; the siderial dates tell you where the Sun actually appears as it moves along its annual path.

March 18 has the same astrological sign in both systems: Pisces.

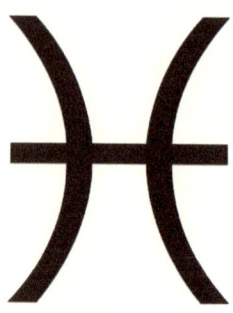

Pisces

Tropical February 20 to March 20

Siderial March 15 to April 14

In the Roman legend of Venus and her son Cupid, they escaped the clutches of Typhon, known as the "father of all monsters," by transforming into fish and tying themselves together with rope. That's why the name Pisces is plural for fish. The constellation appears as a somewhat ragged "V" shape, representing the rope, with the "fish" located at the two rope ends.

In astrology, Pisces is a water sign, compatible with the other water signs Cancer and Scorpio, as well as with the earth signs Taurus, Virgo, and Capricorn. Pisceans are supposed to be imaginative, compassionate, unworldly, secretive, and escapist.

What Day of the Week is March 18?

On what day of the week does March 18 fall?

Surprisingly, this isn't an easy question. Because the calendar year is 365 days long (366 in leap years), it doesn't divide evenly by the seven days of the week.

Also, the Earth goes around the Sun in about 365-1/4 days, so a calendar tends to drift over time. That's why the same date falls on different weekdays in different years.

This is made even more complicated by a change in calendars that took place in 1582. Our modern calendar has its roots in ancient Rome, in a calendar reform conducted by Julius Caesar. Caesar commissioned mathematicians to attack the problem, and came up with the idea of *leap years,* and thus standardized the calendar for centuries to come. This was called the *Julian calendar.*

Over time, however, the small errors in Caesar's calculation compounded. That's why Pope Gregory XIII commissioned the *Gregorian calendar,* used in most of the world today. Some countries converted in 1582, when the calendar was first developed; some converted later; other still haven't changed.

Gregorian and Julian aren't the only types of calendars. The Hebrew year, the Islamic year, and many other calendars are used in different parts of the world and among different people.

You can convert Gregorian dates to other calendars, including the Hebrew calendar, the Islamic calendar, and even the Mayan calendar by visiting the Fourmilab Calendar Converter at http://www.fourmilab.ch/documents/calendar/.

A 50-year brass perpetual calendar.

Copyright, Credit, and Contact

Follow Us

Our blog Dobson's Improbable History features short articles on events and people associated with each day, and updates several times each week. Get the latest on Twitter @SidewiseThinker.

Contact Us

Find an error or a format problem? Want information about the series, about us, or about when the volume for your special day might be available? Please email us at editor@timespinnerpress.com.

Sources and Art Credits

All art and photographs are either in the public domain or used under a Creative Commons license. Attribution is provided where requested by the copyright owner or when of historical significance, listed below.

- The cover photograph of Diamond Head seen from Waikiki Beach, Hawaii, was taken by Daderot, who released it into the public domain.

- The photograph of the Hawaiian islands with labels was retouched from an original satellite picture taken by NASA. It is in the public domain because NASA images are not protected by copyright.

- The flag of Aruba is not an object of copyright.

- The 19th century painting of Jacques de Molay is in the public domain because its copyright is expired. The original is in the collection of the Bibliotheque Nationale de France.

- The 2002 photograph of the Stanley Cup was taken by "Uncleweed" and is used here under the Creative Commons Attribution-Share Alike 2.0 Generic license.

- The 1890 photograph of George I of Greece is in the public domain because its copyright has expired.

- The 1942 photograph of the Mochida family awaiting evacuation to an internment camp was taken by Dorothea Lange and is part of the holdings of the National Archives and Record Service. It is in the public domain as a work of the War Relocation Authority, an agency of the U.S. federal government.

- The patch from the Voskhod 2 mission is not an object of copyright according to the Russian Federation.

- *The Storm on the Sea of Galilee* by Rembrandt is in the public domain because its copyright has expired.

- The 2002 photograph of Vanessa Williams was taken by Angela George, and is used here under the Creative Commons Attribution-Share Alike 3.0 Unported license.

- The 1970 publicity photograph of the *Mission: Impossible* fifth season cast is in the public domain.

- The PR photograph of Edward Everett Horton was taken by James Hargis Connelly. It is in the public domain because it was published between 1923 and 1977 without a copyright notice.

- The image "Street Musicians" by William Johnson is from the Smithsonian American Art Museum, Gift of the Harmon Foundation. No known copyright restrictions on this image exist.

- The 1903 photograph of Nathanael Herreshoff's sloop *Reliance* is from the Detroit Publishing Company collection, donated to the Library of Congress in 1949. According to the Library, there are no known restrictions on the publication of photographs from the collection originally published before 1922.

- The 1981 photograph of Charley Pride was taken by Greg Matheson for the U.S. Department of Defense, and is in the public domain as a work of the U.S. federal government.

- The photograph of Werner Mölders is taken from the German Federal Archives and used here under the Creative Commons Attribution-Share Alike 3.0 Germany license.

- The 1884 political cartoon of Grover Cleveland by Frank Beard was originally published in "The Judge" magazine. It is part of the Library of Congress Print and Picture Collection. It is in the public domain because its copyright has expired.

- The 1849 daguerreotype of John C. Calhoun was taken by Matthew Brady. It is in the public domain because its copyright has expired.

- The photograph of Fess Parker as Daniel Boone from the TV series of the same name is in the public domain because it was published between 1923 and 1977 without a copyright notice.

- The cover of the 1920 issue of *Motion Picture Classic* featuring Wanda Hawley is in the public domain because its copyright has expired.

- The 1880s photograph of the Dakota seen from Central Park is in the public domain because its copyright has expired.

- The 1968 photograph of The Mamas and the Papas from the *Ed Sullivan Show* is in the public domain because it was published between 1923 and 1977 without a copyright notice.

- The detail from the 1897 portrait of Tsar Ivan the Terrible by Viktor M. Vasnetsov is in the public domain because its copyright has expired.

- The illustration of the month of March used on the back cover and in the interior is from the French Gothic illuminated manuscript *Les Très Riches Heures du duc de Berry* by the Limbourg Brothers, Jean Colombe, and an intermediate painter whose name is lost to history. It is in the public domain because its copyright has expired.

- The photograph of aquamarine has been released into the public domain.

- The photograph of daffodils is by Myrabella, and is licensed under the Creative Commons Attribution-Share Alike 3.0 Unported license.

- The 1917 Women's Suffrage demonstration comes from the Library of Congress, Prints and Photographs Division, LC-USZ62-31799 DLC, and is in the public domain because its copyright has expired.

- The 50-year perpetual calendar photograph is in the public domain.